CONTENTS

A baby dog is called a puppy. A newborn puppy cannot see or hear. It uses smell to find its mother and stay close to her. The puppies snuggle up to their mother to keep warm.

The puppies drink their mother's milk. It is full of goodness to help them grow. The mother licks the puppies' fur to keep them clean and to show them that they are safe.

The puppies grow up very fast. When they are about ten days old, their eyes open and they can see. A few days later, their ears open and they can hear, too.

The puppy can stand up now and walk about.
But it is still a bit wobbly. It can bark and wag its tail.
It also starts to get its first sharp, little teeth.

The puppies love playing together. Sometimes they play quite roughly and they pretend to nip and fight. This shows them which puppy is the strongest.

All this playing makes the puppies tired.
They flop down in a heap and go to sleep. Sleep
is very important for them. They need sleep to
help them grow.

The puppies are eight weeks old.
They are growing very fast and
have all their teeth.

They start eating small meals of meat and
biscuits. They have milk and water to drink.

Now the puppies are old enough to leave their mother. They are ready to be chosen as pets. Having a pet dog is fun but you must look after it every day.

At nine weeks old, you need to take your puppy to the vet's. The vet gives the puppy an injection to stop it getting ill. The vet checks that the puppy is healthy.

14

After its injection, the puppy can go outside to play. Puppies like playing in the garden. They race round and round in circles, chasing their tails. They love running after a ball.

Puppies need lots of exercise. This helps their muscles to grow stronger. You should take your puppy out for a walk every day. Your puppy must wear a collar and tag.

By the time it is four months old, the puppy has all of its adult teeth. At home, it needs lots of toys to chew so that it does not chew your shoes!

You need to train your puppy. You can take it a training class. Teach your puppy to come when you call its name and to sit when you tell it to.

Your puppy needs to learn to go to toilet outside. Put some newspaper down. When your puppy needs the toilet, put it on the newspaper. Each time, move the paper closer to the door.

The puppy is a year old. It is a grown-up dog. Male dogs grow bigger than female dogs.

Dogs can live for a long time, usually 10 to 14 years.

The dog is old enough
to have its own puppies. A male and female dog
mate. A few weeks later, the female has puppies.
And the puppies will grow into . . . new dogs!

Index

Further Information

There are many different kinds of dogs. To find out more about dogs and how to look after them as pets, you can visit www.rspca.org.uk (the website of the Royal Society for the Prevention of Cruelty to Animals).